Stop, Thief!

Meg Harper
Illustrated by Heather Heyworth

A & C Black • London

White Wolves series consultant: Sue Ellis,
Centre for Literacy in Primary Education

This book can be used in the White Wolves Guided Reading
programme by readers who need a lot of support in Year 2

First paperback edition 2011
First published 2010 by
A & C Black Publishers Ltd
36 Soho Square, London, W1D 3QY

www.acblack.com

ISBN 978-1-4081-2210-5

Chapter One

Everyone in Jed's family tap-danced.
His mum and his sisters…

Even his dad!

It was all right because no one knew.
Until Jed's dad was in a show…

Then he was in the local paper, wearing silly clothes and his policeman's helmet, tap-dancing.

The bullies at school teased Jed. They hadn't before. Now they tapped their feet whenever he went past.

Now Jed felt too scared to play outside on his bike.

"I don't know what to do," he said.

"You should laugh at them," said Jed's friend, Abe.

"You should ignore them," said Jed's mum. She told Jed's dad all about it.

"Right," said Jed's dad. "I'm going to sort this out."

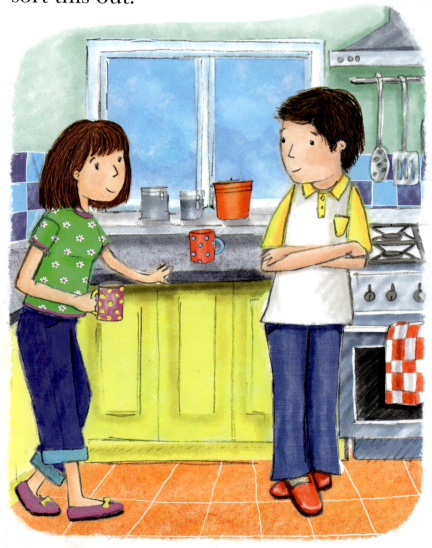

Chapter Two

Jed's dad burst into Jed's bedroom.
He squirted Jed with a water pistol.

"You're coming with me!" he said.

He picked up Jed and threw him over his shoulder.

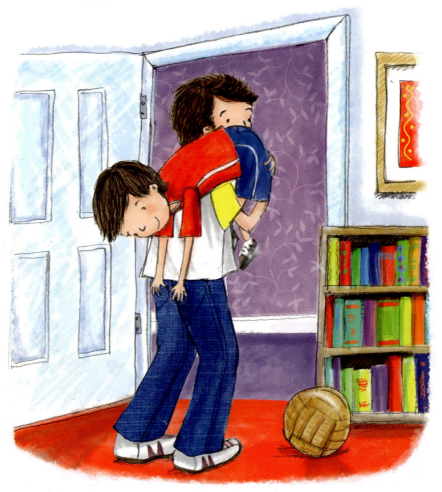

"Where are we going?" squeaked Jed.

"To sort things out," said Jed's dad.

They went outside.

"Get your bike," said Jed's dad. "We're off to the park."

"If you come with me, the bullies will think I'm a wimp," said Jed.

"I'll get a newspaper. Then I'll sit on a bench and look like a spy," said Jed's dad. "Hey! Listen! What's that?"

"What's what?" asked Jed.

"That alarm!" said Jed's dad.

They ran round down the street.

A man burst out of the corner shop.

It had been robbed!

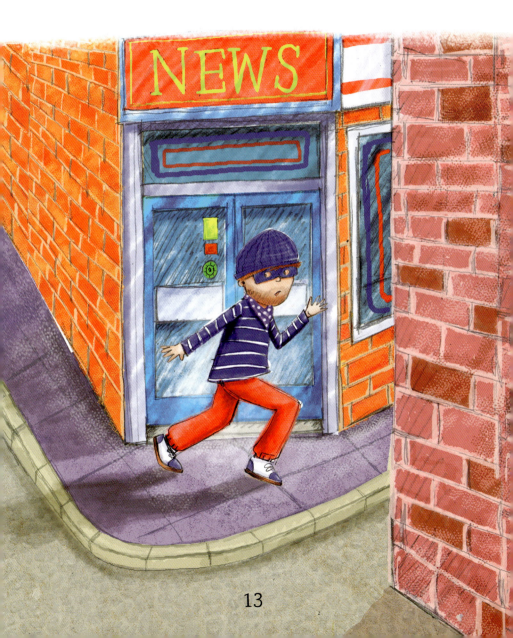

Chapter Three

"Stop, thief!" shouted Jed's dad.
But the man didn't stop.
Jed's dad ran after him.

Jed jumped on his bike.

"Stop, thief!" he yelled, and pedalled after his dad.

People in the street jumped out of
the way.

"Stop, thief!" cried Jed.

The robber banged into a ladder.

A workman dropped his can of paint.

"What's going on?" he asked.

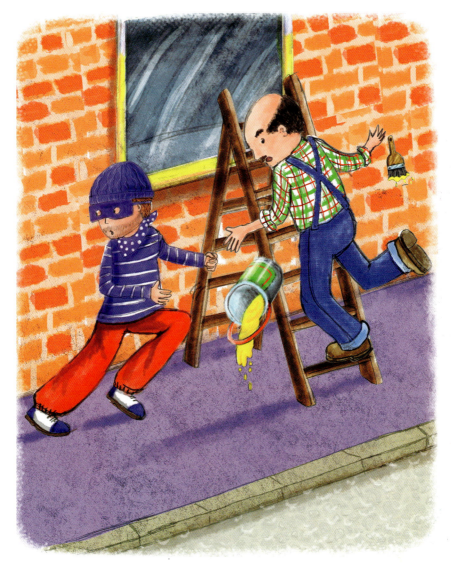

"Stop, thief!" shouted Jed.

So the workman joined in the chase.

Chapter Four

In the park, they nearly ran over a lady with four poodles.

"Watch where you're going!" said the lady.

"Stop, thief!" yelled Jed.

So the lady and the four poodles joined in the chase.

"What's going on?" asked a gardener.

"Stop, thief!" they all shouted.

So the gardener joined in the chase.

And so did a mum with a pram …
and the cook from the café …

and the man cutting the grass.

And then, by the skate park, Jed saw the bullies from school. They stared at him and started laughing.

"What's funny?" cried Jed. "Stop, thief!"

So the bullies joined in the chase.

Chapter Five

They ran and they ran and they ran.
Round the pond …

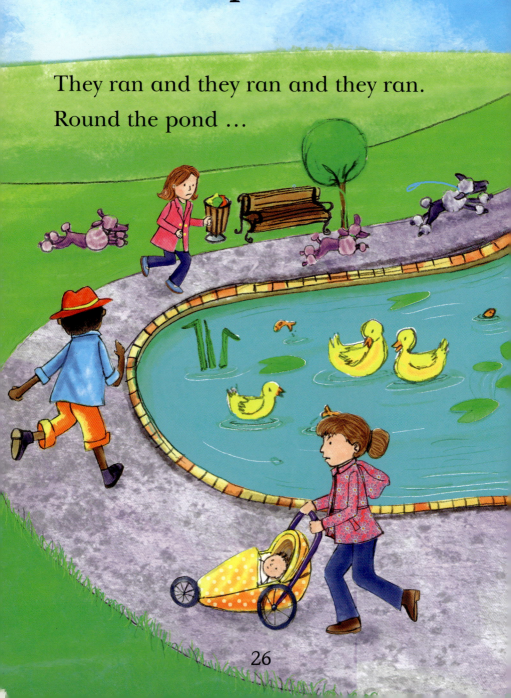

out of the gates …

down the hill …

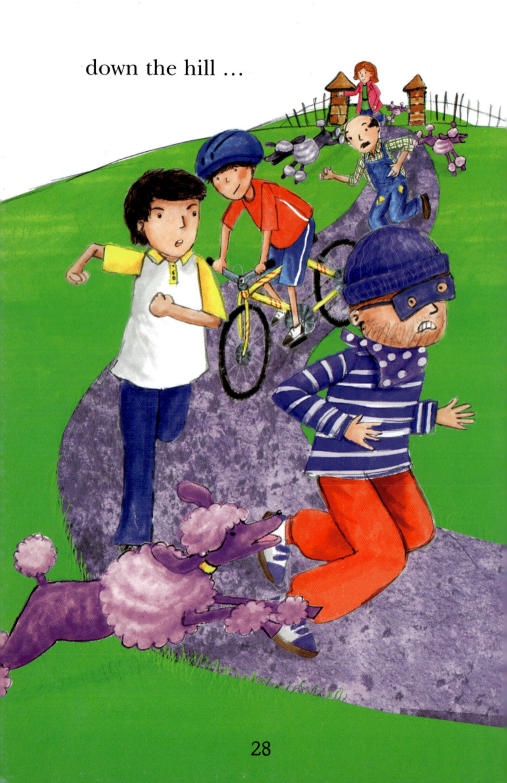

under the railway bridge.

"He'll never do it," gasped the biggest
bully. "He'll never catch him!"

But at that very moment, Jed's dad did! He tripped up the robber with a neat side step, just as another policeman roared up in a police car to help.

They put the robber in the car, while everyone watched.

Jed's dad turned to the bullies. They were still huffing and puffing and red in the face.

"You should take up tap-dancing," he said. "It keeps you very fit."

They didn't.

But Jed did. And now the bullies leave him well alone!